SO-FME-686

Freezer
to
Slow Cooker

Make Life Simpler!

Tired of worrying about what's for dinner? Freezer cooking lets you prep a bunch of homemade meals at one time and freeze them for slow-cooking another day. Everything is ready to go – just pick a bag, thaw, and pop it into your slow cooker to simmer while you're busy with more important things.

The recipes in this book are frozen in gallon-size zippered freezer bags, which hold enough food to feed four or more people. Bags can be frozen flat or upright and will preserve most food combos for up to 3 months. Cook the meals in a 3- to 4-quart slow cooker unless otherwise noted. Prep it, bag it, freeze it, cook it – delicious ready-to-eat dinners can be that simple!

Printed in the United States of America
by G&R Publishing Co.

Distributed By:

507 Industrial Street
Waverly, IA 50677

ISBN-13: 978-1-56383-549-0
Item #7127

Before Prep Day

Clear some level space in your freezer. If you have wire shelves, set cardboard on them to support the bags during freezing. *(After they're solid, store bags flat or upright like books, with all labels facing the same direction.)*

Be sure your freezer is set at the proper temperature *(0° F)*.

Gather these packing supplies: good quality gallon-size zippered freezer bags, permanent marker for labeling bags *(if using paper labels, protect with clear packing tape)*, a container to support the bags during filling, measuring cups and spoons, cutting boards, and sharp knives.

Choose your recipes, make your grocery list *(including freezer bags)*, and buy the necessary items.

On Prep Day

Organize all food, seasonings, and packing supplies.

Label the bag for each meal with cooking instructions, main ingredients *(plus any you will add on cooking day)*, and a use-by date *(usually 3 months from prep day)*.

To support a bag during filling, set it upright in a deep bowl, large measuring cup, pitcher, or even a blender container without the blade. Then fold back the top of the bag to keep it wide open.

Follow recipe directions to combine the food in each bag. Zip the bag closed and knead everything together or gently shake the bag to coat food.

To prevent freezer burn, press out as much air as you can after filling the bag and zip it mostly closed *(leave a small opening)*. Slowly press or roll bag toward the opening to squeeze out remaining air, then zip it closed.

Flatten the bag and place it in the freezer. *(Bags may be stacked to freeze, but put a paper towel between them to prevent sticking.)*

To Cook

Transfer a bag from the freezer to the refrigerator to thaw for 12 to 36 hours *(large quantities of food or chunks of meat thaw more slowly)*. For faster thawing, set the bag in cold water.

You may grease your cooker or use liners designed for slow cooking to make clean-up extra easy.

Dump thawed food into a slow cooker, stir, and put the lid on. Cook as directed and avoid peeking until it's time to check doneness.

To ensure food safety, cook to the following minimum internal temperatures *(but don't over-cook or the meat will dry out)*.

- Whole pieces of beef or pork: 145° *(higher for shredding)*

- All ground meats: 160°

- All poultry: 165° *(legs and thighs will be more tender at 175° to 180°)*

- Casseroles: 165° in the center

Other Tips

Slow cookers vary in their heat, so adjust recommended cooking times for your own cooker *(the ideal fill level is ½ to ⅔ full).*

If your food is still partially frozen when you're ready to cook, increase the cooking time as needed and monitor doneness closely.

In a rush? Start cooking on the high setting, then reduce heat to low after an hour or two. *(Cooking 1 hour on high is similar to 2 hours on low.)*

Less tender cuts of meat tend to cook best on the low setting.

Organize your freezer bags in order of use-by dates and cook the oldest ones first.

Buy meat and produce on sale and pack multiple freezer meals at once to bag some savings. Try bulk cooking ground beef and dividing it among several recipes that call for browned hamburger.

To reduce the cooking liquid or thicken a sauce, remove lid near the end of cooking time or stir in cornstarch and water.

Don't over-stir cheesy or creamy mixtures.

You won't need to blanch the vegetables in most of these recipes.

To preserve the color and texture of green vegetables, add them toward the end of cooking time.

Some foods should not be frozen, including uncooked rice or pasta; cream, sour cream, cottage cheese, and other soft dairy products; raw russet potatoes; and crunchy toppings. These may be successfully stirred in on cooking day or added near the end of cooking time.

Other ingredients and seasonings like salt, pepper, curry powder, onion, citrus zest, celery, and green pepper may lose flavor or taste different after freezing. If you'd prefer not to freeze them, simply add them toward the end of cooking time.

Oriental Tenderloin

1½ to 2 lbs. pork tenderloin

⅓ C. soy sauce

¼ C. olive oil

2 T. Worcestershire sauce

2 T. lemon juice

⅓ C. brown sugar

1 T. dry mustard

1½ tsp. black pepper

2 tsp. minced garlic

Prep & Label Cut the pork into several large chunks to fit your slow cooker. Label a 1-gallon freezer bag with cooking instructions *(see below)* and set the bag upright.

Pack & Freeze Put all liquid ingredients and seasonings into the bag and swirl until mixed. Add the pork, close the bag, and turn a few times to coat meat. Reseal the bag, squeezing out all the air. Freeze flat.

To Cook Thaw. Transfer contents of bag into a slow cooker and cook on low for 3½ to 5 hours or on high for 2 to 3 hours or until meat is done. Let stand a few minutes before slicing.

Try serving with crisp cabbage salad, broccoli slaw, or hot cooked rice.

Freeze up to 3 months

Serves 10

Beef & Barley Soup

1½ lbs. ground beef

1 onion, chopped

2 tsp. each minced garlic, dried basil, and salt

2 T. each dried parsley and sugar

1 tsp. dried thyme

1½ tsp. black pepper

3 celery ribs, sliced

4 medium carrots, peeled & sliced

2 C. frozen green beans

1½ T. Worcestershire sauce

1 C. water

1 T. beef bouillon powder

2 (5.5 oz.) cans V-8 juice

2 (14.5 oz.) cans diced tomatoes

Freeze up to 3 months

On Cooking Day You'll Need 1 C. uncooked barley, 1 (14.5 oz.) can beef broth, 1 C. frozen diced hash browns, 1½ C. water, ½ C. chopped fresh kale or spinach

Prep & Label Cook the ground beef and onion until browned and crumbly; drain. Off the heat, stir in the garlic, basil, salt, parsley, sugar, thyme, and pepper; let cool completely. Meanwhile, label 2 (1-gallon) freezer bags with cooking instructions *(see below)* and set the bags upright.

Pack & Freeze Place half the meat mixture into each bag. Divide the vegetables, Worcestershire sauce, water, and bouillon powder among bags *(it doesn't have to be exactly even)*. Pour 1 can each of juice and diced tomatoes into each bag. Seal the bags well, squeezing out all the air, and clip them together, if you'd like. Freeze flat.

To Cook Thaw both bags. Pour contents of bags into a 4- to 5-quart slow cooker and add the *barley*, *broth*, *hash browns*, and *water*. Cook on low 7 to 8 hours or on high about 4 hours, stirring in *kale* or *spinach* 30 minutes before serving.

To prepare only one freezer bag on cooking day, use a smaller slow cooker and add just ½ C. barley, 1 C. beef broth, ½ C. hash browns, ¾ C. water, and ¼ C. kale or spinach.

Pepper Steak

1½ lbs. boneless beef round steak

1 onion, sliced

2 bell peppers *(any color)*, cut into strips

½ tsp. minced garlic

1 tsp. grated gingerroot

2 T. beef bouillon powder

3 T. soy sauce

1 C. water

On Cooking Day You'll Need 2 T. cornstarch, ¼ C. cold water

Prep & Label Cut the round steak into thin strips about 1½" long. Label a 1-gallon freezer bag with cooking instructions *(see below)* and set the bag upright.

Pack & Freeze Put the beef and all remaining ingredients into the bag and swirl a few times to coat. Squeeze out all the air and seal the bag well. Freeze flat.

To Cook Thaw partially. Pour contents of bag into a slow cooker. Cook on low about 4 hours or until beef is tender. When nearly done, turn cooker to high setting. Dissolve the *cornstarch* in *water* and stir into the beef mixture; cook uncovered for 15 minutes or until thickened.

Tastes great over cooked rice or couscous.

Freeze up to 3 months

11

Thai Lettuce Wraps

1 onion, chopped

½ C. chicken broth

¼ C. soy sauce

1 T. lime juice

2 T. honey

½ C. chunky peanut butter

2 bell peppers *(red, yellow, orange, or combination)*, sliced

4 boneless, skinless chicken breast halves *(about 2 lbs.)*

On Cooking Day You'll Need
large lettuce leaves, ¼ C. crushed peanuts, fresh cilantro *(optional)*

Prep & Label
Label a 1-gallon freezer bag with cooking instructions *(see below)* and set the bag upright.

Pack & Freeze
Combine the onion, broth, soy sauce, lime juice, honey, and peanut butter in the bag and mix it up. Add the bell peppers and chicken; swirl around until well coated. Seal the bag well, pressing out all the air. Freeze flat.

To Cook
Thaw. Dump contents of bag into a slow cooker. Cook on low about 6 hours or on high for 3 to 4 hours. Near the end of cooking time, shred the chicken and cook 15 minutes more. Spoon the meat mixture onto *lettuce leaves* and sprinkle with *peanuts* and *cilantro*, if you'd like. Roll up and enjoy!

Freeze up to 2 months

Serves 6

Curried BBQ Beef

Label a 1-gallon freezer bag with cooking instructions *(see below)* and set the bag upright. Put a 2 lb. boneless beef chuck roast and ¾ lb. shredded carrots into the bag. Add 1 C. ketchup, 2 T. Worcestershire sauce, 4 tsp. brown sugar, 1 T. chili powder, and 1½ tsp. hot sauce. Mix everything together. Reseal the bag, squeezing out all the air. Freeze flat.

On Cooking Day You'll Need 1 to 1½ tsp. curry powder, hamburger buns, mango chutney

To Cook Thaw. Pour contents of bag into a slow cooker and stir in the *curry powder*. Cook for 7 to 8 hours on low, until meat is very tender. Shred the meat and serve on *buns*. Top the beef with some *chutney* for the perfect finish.

Freeze up to 3 months

Serves 6-8

Loaded Chicken & Rice

Label a 1-gallon freezer bag with cooking instructions *(see below)* and set the bag upright. Cook ½ lb. bacon strips until crisp; drain and crumble. Dice 3 boneless, skinless chicken breast halves and 1 (2.5 oz.) pkg. dried beef; add to the bag along with the bacon. Mix in 2 (10.5 oz.) cans cream of chicken soup. Reseal the bag, pressing out all the air. Freeze flat.

On Cooking Day You'll Need 2 C. uncooked instant rice, 2½ C. milk, ½ (8 oz.) block cream cheese *(cubed & softened)*

To Cook Thaw. Dump contents of bag into a 4- to 5-quart slow cooker. Stir in the *uncooked rice* and *milk*. Cook on low 4 to 6 hours or on high 2 to 4 hours, until chicken is done. About 15 minutes before serving, add *cream cheese* and cover to let melt. Stir lightly to combine and serve promptly.

Freeze up to 3 months

15

Turkey-Vegetable Soup

3 large carrots, peeled & sliced into coins

3 small zucchini, cut into bite-size pieces

1 C. chopped onion

1 tsp. minced garlic

1 (15 oz.) can white kidney beans, drained & rinsed

2 (15 oz.) cans tomato sauce

1 T. olive oil

¼ tsp. garlic powder

1 T. Italian seasoning

½ tsp. salt

¼ tsp. black pepper

4 tsp. chicken bouillon powder

1 lb. uncooked ground turkey

Freeze up to 3 months

On Cooking Day You'll Need 3 C. water

Prep & Label Label a 1-gallon freezer bag with cooking instructions *(see below)* and set the bag upright.

Pack & Freeze Put the carrots, zucchini, onion, garlic, and beans into the bag. Pour in the tomato sauce and oil. Add all seasonings and bouillon powder. Crumble the uncooked turkey into the bag last. Squeeze out all the air and seal the bag well. Freeze flat.

To Cook Thaw. Pour contents of bag into a 4- to 5-quart slow cooker and add the water. Cook on high for 1 hour and then reduce heat to low and cook 8 to 10 hours longer, until carrots are tender. Break up the turkey a bit before serving.

Hawaiian Chicken

1 (20 oz.) can pineapple chunks, drained *(reserve ½ C. juice)*

½ C. sugar

½ C. white vinegar

1½ tsp. minced garlic

2 T. soy sauce

4 boneless, skinless chicken breast halves

On Cooking Day You'll Need ciabatta buns or kaiser rolls, sliced Pepper Jack cheese, red onions, barbecue sauce

Prep & Label Label a 1-gallon freezer bag with cooking instructions *(see below)* and set the bag upright.

Pack & Freeze Put the pineapple chunks, reserved juice, sugar, vinegar, garlic, and soy sauce into the bag and swirl to mix. Add the chicken and mix until meat is coated. Reseal the bag, squeezing out all the air. Freeze flat.

To Cook Thaw. Pour contents of bag into a slow cooker. Cook on low about 4 hours or on high for 2 to 3 hours, until chicken is done. Shred the meat or serve whole pieces on toasted *buns* or *rolls*. Top with some of the pineapple chunks and juice from cooker plus a slice of *cheese* and *red onion*. Serve with *barbecue sauce*.

Serves 6-8

Southwest Chili

8 oz. andouille or kielbasa sausage

1 (6 oz.) pkg. Southwestern grilled chicken strips

1 (15 oz.) can Great Northern beans

1 C. chopped onion

1 (10 oz.) can diced tomatoes with green chilies

1 (10.5 oz.) can cream of chicken & mushroom soup

2 tsp. chili powder

1 tsp. each dried oregano and paprika

½ tsp. each black pepper, ground cumin, and garlic powder

¼ tsp. red pepper flakes

1 C. chicken stock

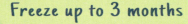

Freeze up to 3 months

On Cooking Day You'll Need 1 (11 oz.) can white shoepeg corn *(drained)*, 8 oz. Velveeta cheese *(cubed)*, corn chips

Prep & Label Label a 1-gallon freezer bag with cooking instructions *(see below)* and set the bag upright. Slice the sausage and cut the chicken strips into bite-size pieces.

Pack & Freeze Put the sausage and chicken into the bag. Add all remaining ingredients and mix everything together. Reseal the bag, pressing out all the air. Freeze flat.

To Cook Thaw. Dump contents of bag into a slow cooker. Cook on low for 6 to 8 hours or on high for 3 to 4 hours. About 30 minutes before serving, stir in the *corn* and *cheese*. Cover and cook until everything is heated through and cheese is melted. Stir and serve with *chips* on top.

To round out this fiesta-worthy meal, serve with a side of fresh fruit and crusty bread.

Caribbean Chicken

3 medium sweet
potatoes, peeled

2½ tsp. minced garlic

1 jalapeño pepper,
chopped

2 T. olive oil

2 T. ground cumin

1 tsp. dried thyme

4 bone-in chicken thighs,
skin removed

Salt

¼ C. orange juice

¼ C. chicken broth

On Cooking Day You'll Need 1 mango, 1 avocado,
1 T. lime juice, pinch of salt

Prep & Label Blanch sweet potatoes in boiling water
for 3 minutes; chill in ice water about 3 minutes. Drain and
cut into ½" slices. In a small food processor, blend garlic,
jalapeño, oil, cumin, and thyme into a thick paste. Label a
1-gallon freezer bag with cooking instructions *(see below)*
and set the bag upright.

Pack & Freeze Sprinkle sweet potatoes and chicken with
salt; coat chicken with the garlic paste. Put potatoes into the bag
and set chicken on top, coating side down. Add orange juice and
broth. Seal bag well, squeezing out all the air. Freeze upright.

To Cook Thaw until chicken thighs can be separated;
remove from bag. Transfer sweet potatoes and liquid into a
slow cooker and set chicken on top, coating side up. Cook on
low 7 to 8 hours or on high 3½ to 4 hours, until chicken is
done. Peel and cube the mango and avocado; toss with lime
juice and salt. Serve over the chicken and sweet potatoes.

Freeze up to 3 months

Broc 'n' Chicken Alfredo

2 lbs. boneless, skinless chicken breasts

1 (14 to 16 oz.) pkg. frozen broccoli florets

1 green bell pepper, diced

½ C. cooked, crumbled bacon *(about 5 strips)*

2 (16 oz.) jars Alfredo sauce

On Cooking Day You'll Need cooked pasta, shredded Parmesan cheese

Prep & Label Cut the chicken into finger-size pieces. Label a 1-gallon freezer bag with cooking instructions *(see below)* and set the bag upright.

Pack & Freeze Put the chicken, broccoli, bell pepper, and bacon into the bag. Pour both jars of sauce over the top and mix until food is evenly coated. Seal the bag well, squeezing out all the air. Freeze flat.

To Cook Thaw. Pour contents of bag into a 4- to 5-quart slow cooker. Cook for 6 to 7 hours on low or 3 to 4 hours on high, just until chicken is done. Stir gently. Serve over hot *pasta* and sprinkle with *Parmesan cheese*.

We used one jar of classic Alfredo sauce and one of roasted garlic Parmesan sauce. Mmmm...good!

Freeze up to 2 months

Serves 4

Bacon 'Shroomed Chops

Label a 1-gallon freezer bag with cooking instructions *(see below)* and set the bag upright. Dump in 1 C. chopped onion, 2 (6.5 oz.) cans mushrooms *(drained)*, ½ C. vegetable broth, 1 (10.75 oz.) can golden mushroom soup, and 1 T. apple cider vinegar. Close the bag and mix everything together. Season 4 (¾"- to 1"-thick) boneless pork chops with salt and black pepper; add the chops to the bag along with ½ C. cooked, crumbled bacon. Reseal the bag, squeezing out all the air. Freeze flat.

To Cook Thaw. Transfer contents of bag into a greased slow cooker. Cook on low for 5 to 6 hours or until chops are done. Spoon some mushroom sauce over the chops before serving.

Freeze up to 3 months

Serves 6

Chili Cheese Fries

Label a 1-gallon freezer bag with cooking instructions *(see below)* and set the bag upright. Crumble 1 lb. uncooked lean ground beef into the bag and add 1 C. chopped onion, 2 to 3 T. chili powder, 2 tsp. ground cumin, 1 (8 oz.) can tomato sauce, 1 (15 oz.) can chili beans, ½ C. water, 1 tsp. Worcestershire sauce, 1 tsp. salt, and ¼ tsp. pepper. Mix well. Reseal bag, squeezing out the air. Freeze flat.

On Cooking Day You'll Need 1 (28 oz.) bag frozen steak fries, 2 C. shredded cheddar cheese, sour cream, green onions

To Cook Thaw. Place *steak fries* around the inside of a 4- to 5-quart slow cooker, leaving a well in the center; pour in contents of bag. Cook 4 to 5 hours on high, until done in the middle. Lightly stir the center after 2 hours. Sprinkle with *cheese* and top with *sour cream* and green onions.

Freeze up to 3 months

Makes 4-6

Flatbread Carnitas

1 C. chopped onion

1 tsp. salt

½ tsp. black pepper

1 tsp. ground cumin

1 tsp. ground oregano

¼ tsp. ground cinnamon

1 (2 to 3 lb.) boneless pork shoulder roast

1 T. minced garlic

1 or 2 chipotles in adobo sauce, chopped

2 C. vegetable broth

Freeze up to 3 months

On Cooking Day You'll Need 4 to 6 flatbread pieces, 1 (15 oz.) can whole kernel corn, sliced jalapeño and/or banana peppers, avocado, 1 (15 oz.) jar white queso dip, fresh cilantro

Prep & Label Label a 1-gallon freezer bag with cooking instructions *(see below)* and set the bag upright.

Pack & Freeze Dump onion into the bag. In a small bowl, mix the salt, pepper, cumin, oregano, and cinnamon; sprinkle over both sides of the roast and rub it in. Set roast into the bag and add the garlic, chipotles, and broth. Seal the bag well, pressing out all the air. Freeze upright.

To Cook Thaw. Transfer contents of bag into a slow cooker. Cook on low for 8 to 10 hours or on high about 5 hours, until meat is done and tender. Discard any netting and shred the pork. Preheat the oven's broiler and warm the *flatbread pieces* on a greased, foil-lined cookie sheet for 5 minutes while broiler heats up. Drain the *corn* and scatter along with shredded meat on each flatbread. Broil 5 to 10 minutes, until lightly browned. Top with *peppers*, *diced avocado*, *warm queso dip*, and *cilantro*. Serve promptly.

You can use this meat for tacos and burritos, too!

Autumn Beef Stew

1 large sweet potato, peeled

2 or 3 medium golden potatoes, peeled

3 medium parsnips, peeled

3 medium carrots, peeled

1½ lbs. beef stew meat, cut into 1" chunks

¼ C. flour

1 tsp. seasoned salt

1 C. frozen whole green beans

1 C. frozen corn

1 tsp. minced garlic

1 (1 oz.) packet dry onion soup mix

3 C. beef broth

On Cooking Day You'll Need salt, black pepper

Prep & Label Cube the sweet potato and golden potatoes; slice the parsnips and carrots into thick coins. Label a 1-gallon freezer bag with cooking instructions *(see below)*. Set the bag upright.

Pack & Freeze Toss the uncooked stew meat into the bag and sprinkle with flour and seasoned salt. Close the bag and shake to coat. Add all the vegetables and remaining ingredients to bag and mix together. Reseal the bag, squeezing out all the air. Freeze flat.

To Cook Thaw. Pour contents of bag into a slow cooker. Cook on low 8 to 10 hours or on high 4 to 6 hours, until meat and vegetables are tender. Season with *salt* and *pepper* to taste.

Freeze up to 3 months

Serves 8

BBQ Beef Brisket

½ C. ketchup

½ C. chili sauce

¼ C. brown sugar

½ tsp. dry mustard

2 T. white vinegar

2 T. Worcestershire sauce

1½ tsp. liquid smoke

1 tsp. chili powder

½ tsp. garlic powder

¼ tsp. celery seed

⅛ tsp. black pepper

1 (3 lb.) beef brisket

Freeze up to 3 months

On Cooking Day You'll Need your favorite barbecue sauce

Prep & Label Label a 1-gallon freezer bag with cooking instructions *(see below)* and set the bag upright.

Pack & Freeze Pour the ketchup, chili sauce, brown sugar, dry mustard, vinegar, Worcestershire sauce, and liquid smoke into the bag and mix everything together. In a small bowl, stir together the chili powder, garlic powder, celery seed, and pepper. Sprinkle seasoning mixture over the brisket and rub it in well. Place brisket into the bag and swirl until meat is evenly coated. Reseal the bag, pressing out all the air. Freeze flat.

To Cook Thaw. Transfer brisket and sauce into a 4- to 5-quart slow cooker. Cook on low for 8 to 10 hours or until tender. Remove meat from cooker and slice across the grain; discard the sauce in cooker and serve the meat with *barbecue sauce.*

Tastes perfect with side dishes like potato salad, baked beans, or broccoli-grape salad.

Saucy Meatballs

1½ lbs. lean ground beef

1 (4.25 oz.) can deviled ham

1 (5 oz.) can evaporated milk

1 egg, slightly beaten

2 T. dried minced onion

2 C. soft bread crumbs

¼ C. dry Italian bread crumbs

1 tsp. salt

¼ tsp. black pepper

1 tsp. garlic powder

1 (28 oz.) can crushed tomatoes

1 (6 oz.) can tomato paste

1 (8 oz.) can tomato sauce

1 C. chopped onion

1 T. brown sugar

2 tsp. each minced garlic and dried oregano

1 tsp. dried thyme

1 (6 oz.) can sliced mushrooms, drained

On Cooking Day You'll Need cooked pasta, shredded Parmesan cheese

Prep & Label Label a 1-gallon freezer bag with cooking instructions *(see below)* and set the bag upright.

Pack & Freeze Mix ground beef, ham, milk, egg, onion, all bread crumbs, salt, pepper, and garlic powder; shape into 2″ meatballs. Freeze on cookie sheets about 1 hour. Meanwhile, pour crushed tomatoes and all remaining ingredients into bag; mix well. Add frozen meatballs and swirl gently to coat. Reseal the bag, pressing out all the air. Freeze flat.

To Cook Thaw partially and add to a 4- to 5-quart slow cooker. Cook 7 to 9 hours on low or until meatballs are done. Serve over hot *pasta* and top with *Parmesan cheese.*

Freeze up to 3 months

Steak Fajitas

1½ lbs. sirloin strip steak, cut into thin strips

3 bell peppers *(any color)*, cut into strips

1 C. frozen chopped onions

2 tsp. minced garlic

2 tsp. dried cilantro

1½ tsp. chili powder

1½ tsp. ground cumin

1½ tsp. ground coriander

1½ tsp. salt

½ tsp. black pepper

1 C. chunky salsa

Generous splash of lime juice

On Cooking Day You'll Need large flour tortillas, sour cream, 1 avocado, diced tomatoes, fresh cilantro

Prep & Label Label a 1-gallon freezer bag with cooking instructions *(see below)* and set the bag upright.

Pack & Freeze Place the steak and all remaining ingredients into the bag; mix gently. Reseal the bag, pressing out all the air. Freeze flat.

To Cook Thaw. Dump contents of bag into a slow cooker and cook on low 5 to 6 hours or on high about 3 hours, until meat is tender. With a slotted spoon, scoop meat mixture onto *tortillas* and top with *sour cream*, *diced avocado*, *tomatoes*, and *cilantro* as desired.

Freeze up to 3 months

Serves 3-6

Apricot Chicken

Label a 1-gallon freezer bag with cooking instructions *(see below)* and set the bag upright. Dump in 1 (12 oz.) jar apricot preserves and add 1 tsp. dried minced onion, 1 T. Dijon mustard, 1 T. soy sauce, ¼ tsp. ground ginger, and ½ tsp. red pepper flakes. Mix everything together. Add 6 large chicken thighs and/or legs to the bag *(about 4 lbs.)* and shake until chicken is evenly coated. Reseal the bag, pressing out all the air. Freeze flat.

To Cook Thaw. Empty contents of bag into a 4- to 5-quart slow cooker and cook 5 to 6 hours on low or 3 to 4 hours on high, until chicken is done. Couscous and stir-fry veggies complete this meal deliciously.

38 Freeze up to 3 months

Makes 12

Tangy Sloppy Joes

Label 2 (1-gallon) freezer bags with cooking instructions *(see below)* and set upright. In a skillet, brown 3 lbs. ground beef until crumbly; drain and let cool. Meanwhile, put these ingredients into each bag: ½ C. chopped onion, ½ diced red or green bell pepper, ½ (15 oz.) can tomato sauce, ⅓ C. ketchup, 1½ tsp. Worcestershire sauce, 1 tsp. chili powder, and ¼ tsp. each black pepper and garlic powder. Add half the meat *(about 3¾ C.)* to each bag and mix well. Reseal bags, press flat, and freeze.

On Cooking Day You'll Need hamburger buns, condiments

To Cook Thaw one *(or both)* bags. Transfer into a slow cooker and cook on low 6 to 8 hours or on high 2 to 4 hours. *(If cooking both bags together, use the longer cook times.)* Spoon meat mixture onto *buns* and add any *condiments* you like.

Freeze up to 3 months

39

Serves 4

Crockin' Salmon Packs

¼ C. brown sugar

2 tsp. paprika

2 tsp. ground cumin

2 tsp. minced garlic

1 tsp. dried oregano

1 tsp. salt

½ to 1 tsp. cayenne pepper

4 (4 oz.) fresh salmon fillets*

2 (10 oz.) pkgs. frozen rice blend with vegetables

Fresh asparagus, optional

*If using frozen salmon, do not thaw.

Freeze up to 3 months

Prep & Label Label a 1-gallon zippered freezer bag with cooking instructions *(see below)* and set the bag upright. Cut 4 (15") lengths of foil.

Pack & Freeze Mix together the brown sugar and all seasonings. Coat both sides of salmon fillets with the seasoning mixture, patting it in place. Divide the rice blend evenly among the foil pieces and set a fillet on top of each. If you'd like, add some asparagus spears to each pack. Wrap the foil around the food and seal well to make four separate packs. Place the packs inside the labeled bag and zip closed, pressing out the air. Freeze.

To Cook Thaw partially. Layer the foil packs in a 4- to 5-quart slow cooker. Cover and cook on high for 2 to 3 hours or until fish is flaky and rice is tender.

Try serving with warm biscuits and sweet honey-butter. Yum-o!

Lazy Day Tostadas

1½ lbs. lean ground beef

2 (15 oz.) cans refried beans

1 (1 oz.) packet taco seasoning

1 tsp. chili powder

1 tsp. ground cumin

1 (8 oz.) can tomato sauce

½ C. water

On Cooking Day You'll Need crisp tostada shells, 1½ C. shredded Mexican cheese blend, lettuce, diced tomatoes, sliced black olives, sour cream, avocados, salsa

Prep & Label Label a 1-gallon freezer bag with cooking instructions *(see below)* and set the bag upright.

Pack & Freeze Crumble the uncooked ground beef into the bag and add all remaining ingredients. Mash everything together until well mixed. Reseal the bag, pressing out all the air. Freeze flat.

To Cook Thaw. Add contents of bag to a slow cooker. Cook 6 to 7 hours on low, stirring to break up the meat halfway through cooking time. Spread the hot mixture on *tostada shells* and top with *cheese, lettuce, tomatoes, olives, sour cream, diced avocado*, and *salsa* as desired.

Serves 8

Shortcut Lasagna

- 1 lb. Italian turkey sausage
- 1 (15 oz.) can tomato sauce
- 1 (14.5 oz.) can diced tomatoes
- 1 (6 oz.) can tomato paste
- 1 C. water
- 1 tsp. salt
- ½ tsp. black pepper
- ½ tsp. garlic powder
- 2 tsp. Italian seasoning

Enjoy delicious lasagna anytime without heating up your oven — genius!

Freeze up to 3 months

On Cooking Day You'll Need 12 oz. uncooked lasagna noodles, 1 (12 oz.) carton cottage cheese, 4 C. shredded mozzarella cheese, ½ C. grated Parmesan cheese

Prep & Label In a skillet, brown the sausage until crumbly; drain and let cool. Meanwhile, label a 1-gallon freezer bag with cooking instructions *(see below)* and set the bag upright.

Pack & Freeze Toss the meat into bag with all remaining ingredients; mix well. Reseal the bag, press flat, and freeze.

To Cook Thaw. Spread ¼ of the meat sauce *(about 1½ C.)* in a 4- to 5-quart slow cooker and set ⅓ of the *lasagna noodles* on top, breaking as needed to fit. Top with ½ C. *cottage cheese*, 1 C. *mozzarella*, and 2 T. *Parmesan*. Make two more layers of meat sauce, noodles, and cheeses. Top with a final layer of noodles and remaining meat sauce. Cook 4 to 5 hours on low, until pasta is tender. Sprinkle with the remaining 1 C. *mozzarella*; cover and let melt. Top with remaining 2 T. *Parmesan cheese* before serving.

Cajun Combo

1 lb. boneless, skinless chicken breasts, diced

1 (14 to 16 oz.) pkg. andouille or smoked sausage, sliced

2 C. chopped onion

2 C. sliced celery

1 (14.5 oz.) can diced tomatoes

⅓ C. tomato paste

1 (14.5 oz.) can chicken broth

1 tsp. minced garlic

1 to 2 tsp. Cajun seasoning

On Cooking Day You'll Need 1⅔ C. uncooked instant brown rice, ¾ C. chopped green bell pepper, salt, 12 oz. frozen raw shrimp *(peeled & deveined)*

Prep & Label Label a 1-gallon freezer bag with cooking instructions *(see below)* and set the bag upright.

Pack & Freeze Put the chicken, sausage, onion, and celery into the bag. Add all remaining ingredients and mix together well. Reseal the bag, pressing out all the air. Freeze flat.

To Cook Thaw. Transfer contents of bag into a 4- to 5-quart slow cooker. Cook 4 to 5 hours on low or 2 to 3 hours on high, until chicken is just done. With the cooker on the high setting, stir in *uncooked rice* and *bell pepper*. Cover and cook 30 minutes more, until most of the liquid is absorbed and rice is tender. Season with *salt*. Stir in the *shrimp* and cook 2 to 3 minutes longer, until shrimp are pink and heated through.

Freeze up to 3 months

Manhattan Clam Chowder

5 bacon strips, diced

1 onion, chopped

2 celery ribs, sliced

2 medium carrots, peeled & sliced

3 medium golden potatoes, peeled & cubed

1 T. dried parsley

½ tsp. salt

¼ tsp. black pepper

1 bay leaf

1½ tsp. dried thyme

1 (28 oz.) can diced tomatoes

1 (8 oz.) bottle clam juice

On Cooking Day You'll Need 1 or 2 (10 oz.) cans baby clams, croutons

Prep & Label In a skillet, cook the bacon, onion, and celery until bacon is golden brown and vegetables are tender. Drain and let cool; discard the grease. Label a 1-gallon freezer bag with cooking instructions *(see below)* and set the bag upright.

Pack & Freeze Dump the bacon mixture and all remaining ingredients into the bag; mix everything together. Seal the bag well, squeezing out all the air. Freeze flat.

To Cook Thaw. Pour contents of bag into a slow cooker. Cook about 5½ hours on low. Stir in the *clams* with ¼ cup of their liquid; cover and cook 30 minutes more or until heated through. Remove the bay leaf and top with *croutons* before serving.

Freeze up to 3 months

Serves 4-6

Honey Chicken Strips

Label a 1-gallon freezer bag with cooking instructions *(see below)* and set the bag upright. Combine 1 C. honey, ½ C. soy sauce, 2 T. chopped onion, ¼ C. ketchup, 2 T. vegetable oil, 1½ tsp. minced garlic, ½ tsp. red pepper flakes, and 2 lbs. boneless, skinless chicken breast strips in the bag. Mix until coated. Reseal the bag, pressing out all the air. Freeze flat.

On Cooking Day You'll Need flour tortillas, shredded lettuce, sliced red onion, sliced tomatoes

To Cook Thaw and dump into a slow cooker. Cook on low 4 hours or on high 2 to 3 hours, until done. Arrange chicken *(drained)* down center of *tortillas* and top with *lettuce, onion,* and *tomatoes*. Roll up and serve with remaining sauce.

50

Freeze up to 3 months

Serves 4

Italian Beef Subs

Label a 1-gallon freezer bag with cooking instructions *(see below)* and set the bag upright. Place 1 (2 lb.) beef chuck roast into the bag and add 1 (16 oz.) bag frozen California blend veggies *(broccoli, cauliflower, carrots)*, 3 T. olive oil, 2 T. red wine vinegar, ½ tsp. salt, ¼ tsp. black pepper, and 1 tsp. each minced garlic, onion powder, dried thyme, dried basil, and dried oregano. Mix well. Reseal bag, pressing out the air. Freeze flat.

On Cooking Day You'll Need Italian rolls, sliced jalapeño and/or banana peppers, provolone cheese slices *(optional)*

To Cook Thaw. Empty contents of bag into a slow cooker and cook 6 to 8 hours on low or until tender. Thinly slice the meat. Arrange meat and vegetables on *rolls* and top with *peppers* and *cheese* as desired.

Freeze up to 3 months

Serves 8-10

Taco Chicken Soup

1½ lbs. boneless, skinless chicken breasts, diced

1 onion, chopped

½ C. grated carrots

1 (15 oz.) can black beans, drained & rinsed

1 (15 oz.) can navy beans, drained & rinsed

1 C. frozen corn

1 (8 oz.) can tomato sauce or juice

2 (10 oz.) cans diced tomatoes with green chilies

1 (1 oz.) packet taco seasoning

Freeze up to 3 months

On Cooking Day You'll Need
12 oz. beer *(or chicken broth)*, salt, black pepper, sour cream, shredded Mexican cheese blend, green onions, tortilla chips

Prep & Label
Label a 1-gallon freezer bag with cooking instructions *(see below)* and set the bag upright.

Pack & Freeze
Dump all ingredients into the bag and mix well. Reseal the bag, pressing out all the air. Freeze flat.

To Cook
Thaw. Add contents of bag to a 4- to 5-quart slow cooker and stir in the *beer* (or *broth*). Cook on low 8 to 9 hours or on high 5 to 6 hours. Season with *salt* and *pepper*. Top with *sour cream*, *cheese*, *green onions*, and *chips* before serving.

Serves 4

Hambuger Chow Mein

Label a 1-gallon freezer bag with cooking instructions *(see below)* and set the bag upright. Crumble 1 lb. uncooked lean ground beef into the bag and add 1 diced onion, 2 sliced celery ribs, and 1 (10.7 oz.) can cream of mushroom soup; mix well. Add 1 (10.5 oz.) can chicken noodle soup, 1 (14 to 15 oz.) can mixed Chinese vegetables *(drained)*, 1 chopped green or red bell pepper, 1 tsp. soy sauce, ½ tsp. salt, and ¼ tsp. black pepper; mix gently. Reseal the bag, pressing out all the air. Freeze flat.

On Cooking Day You'll Need crisp chow mein noodles

To Cook Thaw. Add contents of bag to a slow cooker. Cook on high for 3½ to 5 hours or until meat is done. Serve over *chow mein noodles.*

54

Freeze up to 3 months

Serves 5

Cheesy Potato Soup

Label a 1-gallon freezer bag with cooking instructions *(see below)* and set the bag upright. Dump in 1 (28 oz.) bag frozen diced O'Brien hash browns and add 2 C. each diced ham and frozen broccoli florets, 1½ C. chopped onion, 1 (10.5 oz.) can cream of potato soup, 1 (10.5 oz.) can broccoli cheese soup, and 1 tsp. each garlic powder and black pepper. Pour 1 (14.5 oz.) can chicken broth over everything and mix lightly. Reseal bag, pressing out the air. Freeze flat.

On Cooking Day You'll Need 2 C. shredded cheddar cheese

To Cook Thaw. Pour contents of bag into a greased slow cooker. Cook on low about 5 hours or until potatoes are tender. Lightly stir in the *cheese*; cover and cook 30 to 45 minutes longer, until cheese is melted. Stir just before serving.

Freeze up to 6 weeks

Serves 8

Tomato Tortellini Soup

2 T. olive oil

1 onion, chopped

1 T. minced garlic

1 (10 oz.) pkg. frozen spinach

1 (28 oz.) can tomato sauce

1 (28 oz.) can crushed tomatoes

1 tsp. dried basil

1 tsp. dried oregano

1 tsp. black pepper

2 tsp. salt

Freeze up to 3 months

On Cooking Day You'll Need 3½ C. water, 1 (20 oz.) pkg. frozen cheese tortellini, shredded Parmesan cheese, fresh basil

Prep & Label Heat the oil in a skillet and sauté the onion until tender. Stir in the garlic and let cool. Meanwhile, label a 1-gallon freezer bag with cooking instructions *(see below)* and set the bag upright.

Pack & Freeze Put the block of frozen spinach into the bag and add the tomato sauce, crushed tomatoes, onion mixture, and all seasonings; give it a few swirls until combined. Reseal the bag, pressing out all the air. Freeze flat.

To Cook Thaw. Add contents of bag to a 4- to 5-quart slow cooker along with the *water*. Cook for 6 to 8 hours on low or 3 to 4 hours on high. Stir in the *frozen tortellini* and cook covered on high for 15 to 30 minutes longer or until pasta is done. Top with *Parmesan cheese* and *basil* before serving.

Remember to date and label all your bags of soup. Soups tend to look the same once frozen so you'll be glad you did!

Serves 4

BBQ Ribs & Taters

3 lbs. pork baby back ribs

½ C. apple juice

1½ tsp. salt

1 tsp. black pepper

1½ C. ketchup

1 T. Worcestershire sauce

¾ C. brown sugar

2 T. apple cider vinegar

2 tsp. minced garlic

Serve up those sweet taters topped with butter and cinnamon & sugar – yum!

58

Freeze up to 3 months

On Cooking Day You'll Need parchment paper *(double layer)*, 4 medium sweet or baking potatoes, foil

Prep & Label Cut ribs into four serving-size pieces. Label a 1-gallon and a 1-quart freezer bag with cooking instructions *(see below)* and set the bags upright.

Pack & Freeze Place ribs into the gallon bag. Add juice, salt, and pepper. Mix to coat the meat and seal bag, pressing out all the air; set aside. In the quart bag, mix ketchup and all remaining ingredients. Reseal the bag, pressing out the air. Clip bags together and freeze flat.

To Cook Thaw both bags. Dump gallon bag into a 4- to 5-quart slow cooker and set *parchment paper* over ribs. Pierce *potato*es and wrap in *foil*; set them on the paper. Cook on low 7 to 8 hours. Remove potatoes and paper. With a turkey baster, drain liquid from slow cooker and discard. Pour sauce from quart bag over ribs in cooker; cover. Set potatoes on lid to keep warm. Cook on high 30 to 60 minutes longer.

Serves 6-8

Nacho Tater Tot Bake

Label a 1-gallon freezer bag with cooking instructions *(see below)* and set the bag upright. Crumble 1 lb. uncooked pork sausage into the bag and add 1 (10.75 oz.) can nacho cheese soup, 1 (3 oz.) pkg. real bacon bits, ½ C. chopped onion, 1 chopped green bell pepper, 1 C. frozen corn, ¼ tsp. each salt and black pepper, ¼ C. milk, 1 C. shredded mozzarella cheese, and 1 T. Sriracha sauce. Mix well. Reseal the bag, pressing out all the air. Freeze flat.

On Cooking Day You'll Need 1 (32 oz.) bag frozen tater tots, 1 C. shredded Colby-Jack cheese

To Cook Thaw. Layer *tater tots* over the bottom and up the side of a 4- to 5-quart slow cooker and add contents of bag. Cook 4 to 5 hours on high or until done in the center. Before serving, sprinkle with *cheese*.

Freeze up to 3 months

Serves 8

Meatball Stroganoff

Label a 1-gallon freezer bag with cooking instructions *(see below)* and set the bag upright. Dump 1 (24 to 26 oz.) pkg. fully cooked frozen meatballs, 1 C. chopped onion, 2 (10.7 oz.) cans cream of mushroom soup, and 8 oz. sliced fresh mushrooms into the bag and mix everything together. Seal the bag well, squeezing out all the air. Freeze flat.

On Cooking Day You'll Need 1 (8 oz.) pkg. cream cheese *(cubed & softened)*, 1 C. sour cream, cooked egg noodles

To Cook Thaw. Transfer contents of bag into a slow cooker and cook on low for 5 to 7 hours, until fully cooked. During the last 45 minutes of cooking time, gently stir in the *cream cheese* and *sour cream* and let melt. Stir again and serve promptly over hot *noodles*.

Freeze up to 2 months

Chicken Cordon Bleu

4 boneless, skinless
  chicken breast halves

4 slices deli-style ham

4 slices Swiss or
  provolone cheese

Salt and black pepper
  to taste

4 bacon strips

On Cooking Day You'll Need ¼ C. water, ⅓ C. apple juice, 1 tsp. chicken bouillon powder, ½ C. shredded white processed cheese *(like provel or American)*, 1 to 2 T. milk, croutons *(crushed)*

Prep & Label Place chicken between two pieces of plastic wrap and flatten with a smooth meat mallet until ¼" thick. Label a 1-gallon freezer bag with cooking instructions *(see below)*.

Pack & Freeze Set a slice of ham and cheese on each chicken piece. Season with salt and pepper. Roll up chicken, tucking in ends to enclose cheese. Wrap with a bacon strip and secure with toothpicks. Slide rolls into the bag and seal, pressing out the air without poking holes in bag. Insert into a second bag, seal, and freeze flat.

To Cook Thaw. Arrange chicken rolls in a 4- to 5-quart slow cooker. Mix *water*, *apple juice* and *bouillon powder*; pour over chicken. Cook on high 2 to 3 hours. Before serving, combine *processed cheese* and 1 T. *milk* and microwave on high about 20 seconds; stir. Microwave in 10-second spurts until melted and smooth, stirring in more milk as needed. Sprinkle with *croutons*, slice chicken into rounds, and drizzle with cheese sauce.

Freeze up to 2 months

Index